Hockey
CHALLENGE

Puzzles, Quizzes, Games and Other Cool Stuff for Young Sports Fans

Kathy Vanderlinden

GREYSTONE BOOKS

Douglas & McIntyre
Vancouver/Toronto

Greystone Books
A division of Douglas & McIntyre Ltd.
1615 Venables Street
Vancouver, British Columbia
V5L 2H1

Canadian Cataloguing in Publication Data

Vanderlinden, Kathy.
  Hockey challenge

  ISBN 1-55054-645-7

  1. Hockey–Juvenile literature. I. Title.
GV847.25.V36 1998   j796.962   C98-910774-4

Front cover illustration and text illustrations by Rose Cowles
Cover and text design by Rose Cowles
Printed and bound in Canada by Transcontinental Printing and Graphics

Kathy Vanderlinden is a Toronto editor and writer with an extensive
background in children's literature. She would like to thank Kerry Banks
and Sarah Ellis for their careful reviews of the manuscript and useful
suggestions, and James Little and Stewart Vanderlinden for their helpful tips.

The publisher gratefully acknowledges the assistance of the Canada
Council and of the British Columbia Ministry of Tourism,
Small Business and Culture. The publisher also acknowledges
the financial support of the Government of Canada through the
Book Publishing Industry Development Program for its publishing activities.

Contents

Introduction

If you're reading this book, you probably love hockey. Maybe you play the game yourself. Or maybe you like to watch your favorite teams in action. Either way, you know hockey is just about the coolest game going.

Hockey is not easy. It demands skill, power, determination, and nerve. To master it means getting up before dawn in the winter cold and practicing tricky moves for hours—for years on end. Yet hundreds of thousands of Canadian kids have been doing that happily for generations. Organized hockey is more than 120 years old in North America. And today hockey is played all over the world.

Hockey's got everything—speed, danger, suspense, and showmanship. Fans know the thrill of watching the pros as they fly down the ice on breakaways, make lightning passes, slam in spectacular goals—and crash into pileups at the boards. For kids who play, the thrills are simpler. Getting suited up for the first time in that take-no-prisoners uniform. Practicing until you finally get off the perfect slapshot. Celebrating a hard win with your teammates. At any level, hockey is great fun.

This book is for kids who can't get enough hockey. You've watched, you've played—now it's time to puzzle. You don't have to be a walking hockey-fact book. These quizzes will test your knowledge of the game, but often you just have to follow the clues, use common sense, and be a smart guesser. So find a pencil, step up to the face-off circle, and get ready to score some goals.

the rink →

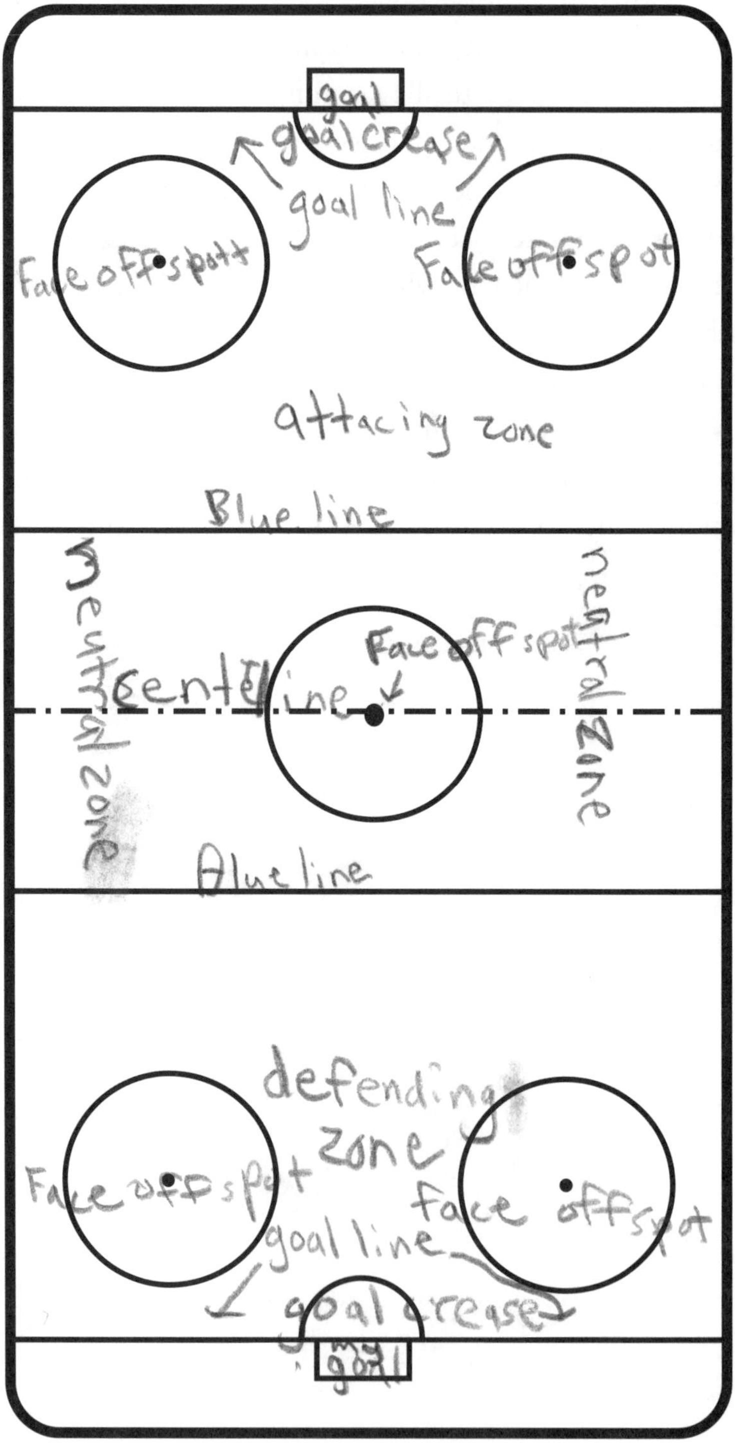

goal

← goal crease →

goal line

Face off spot   Face off spot

attacing zone

Blue line

neutral zone   center line   Face off spot →   neutral zone

Blue line

defending zone

Face off spot   face off spot

goal line

← goal crease →

goal

Rink-O-Rama

Here's where it all happens—on the ice rink. Games are a lot more exciting when you know what all those red and blue lines, circles, and dots mean. How many parts of a hockey rink can you name? In this warm-up quiz, choose labels from the list below and write them beside the right parts in the diagram.

blue line   face-off spot

centerline   center-ice circle

neutral zone   goal

defending zone   goal crease

attacking zone   goal line

the player

Team Plays

In North America, the best professional hockey players compete in the National Hockey League, or NHL. The league has nearly 30 teams. Every season these teams fight the mightiest hockey battles and strive for the greatest hockey prize, the Stanley Cup. Some teams, such as the Montreal Canadiens, have been around since the NHL began, while others are brand-new. Can you tag these teams?

1. Draw lines to connect these Canadian cities with their NHL teams.

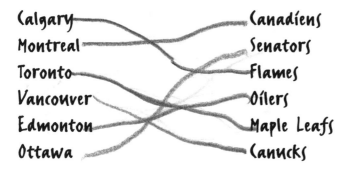

Calgary — Canadiens
Montreal — Senators
Toronto — Flames
Vancouver — Oilers
Edmonton — Maple Leafs
Ottawa — Canucks

2. OK, if that was too easy, try this one. Which American teams wear the crests shown on the next page? Choose the names from the list below and write them on the lines.

Pittsburgh Penguins   Detroit Red Wings
Chicago Blackhawks   New Jersey Devils
Boston Bruins   Buffalo Sabres

a) <u>Buffalo sabers</u>   b) <u>New Jersey Devils</u>

c) <u>Detroit Red Wings</u> d) <u>Boston Bryins</u>

e) <u>Pitsburg Penguins</u>   f) <u>Chicago Blackhawks</u>

3

Game 3

Playing by the Rules

Like every game, hockey has a bunch of rules. Some rules describe the game and tell you how to play it, and others help to make the game faster, safer, or fairer. In this quiz, the rules are simple. Just pick out the Do's and Don'ts of hockey.

1. Which of the following are NHL hockey rules?

YES NO (a) A red light signals the end of a period or game.

YES NO (b) The pucks must be frozen before each game.

YES NO (c) The ice rink should be 61 meters by 26 meters (200 feet by 85 feet).

YES NO (d) A game has two periods of 30 minutes each.

YES NO (e) The rink is surrounded by a fence ("boards") about 2.5 meters (eight feet) high.

YES NO (f) Rinks must have a separate penalty area for each team.

2. Which of these actions could send a player to the penalty box (or stop play)?

YES NO (a) Catching the puck

YES NO (b) Throwing your stick at the puck.

YES NO (c) Holding onto a player to stop him or her from scoring

YES NO (d) Playing without a helmet

4

YES | **NO** (e) Carrying your stick above shoulder height

YES | **NO** (f) Falling on the puck to stop play

YES | **NO** (g) Wearing a glove with a hole cut out of the palm

YES | **NO** (h) Shooting the puck from your end to the opposite end of the ice

YES | **NO** (i) Skating ahead of the puck into the opposing team's zone

YES | **NO** (j) Starting a fight while wearing a face shield

Always Raising the Bar

In 1944–45, when Canadiens' Maurice (Rocket) Richard scored 50 goals in one season—the first time in NHL history—it was considered an incredible feat. Since then, more than 130 NHL players have hit that mark, and some have gone much higher. The 50-goal season is now considered a standard of offensive excellence.

Hockey Lingo

If you play the game, you have to talk the talk. Here are some terms to show you know your way around a hockey arena. Pick the right definitions:

1. Slapshot

(a) A shot that causes the puck to hit the goalie's face

(b) A shot that bounces off the board

(c) A fast, powerful shot made with a swinging stroke

(d) A low shot made by snapping the wrists

2. Zamboni

(a) A popular snack sold at hockey games

(b) The first Italian-born player in the NHL

(c) A backhand shot

(d) An ice-cleaning machine

3. Hat trick

(a) A player plays without a helmet.

(b) A player scores three times in a game.

(c) The puck is passed three times before a goal is scored.

(d) Fans throw their hats in the air when their team scores.

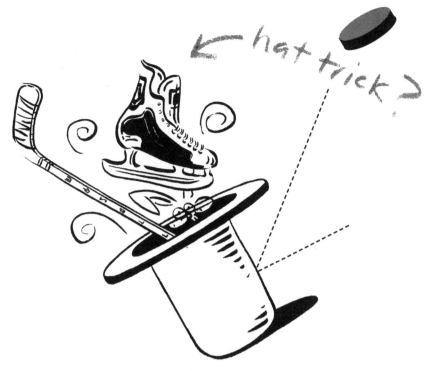

4. **Blocker**

(a) The goalie's extra-wide stick

(b) A successful defensive play

(c) The glove a goalie wears on his stick hand

(d) A defenseman

5. **Stickhandle**

(a) The shaft of a hockey stick

(b) The blade of a hockey stick

(c) To maneuver the puck with your stick

(d) To check another player with your stick

Cross-Check

This crossword is all about plays, teams, and players. Work out the words from the clues and then write them in the appropriate places in the diagram.

Acro∫∫

1. Goalies try to _ _ _ _ the puck.
3. When stickhandling, keep your head _ _.
4. Philadelphia Flyers center _ _ _ _ Lindros.
6. Hockey father and _ _ _Bobby and Brett Hull.
8. Let's go to the hockey _ _ _ _!

9. It's OK to _ _ _ _ the puck but not another player.

10. You should _ _ your best to play well.

12. Nickname for Montreal Canadiens: _ _ _ _.

14. Three to get ready, and _ _ _ _ to go!

16. Get the puck _ _ the net.

17. Cold _ _ ice.

18. Hockey players skate _ _ _ _.

20. Pucks are _ _ _ _-shaped.

21. Record the game on an _ _ _ _ _ -tape.

23. Goalies find that _ _ _ _ _ _ to wear masks. (2 words)

25. Where TV newscasters discuss the game: in the _ _ _ _ _ _.

27. The Winnipeg _ _ _ _.

28. The stands are filled with _ _ _ _ _ _.

Down

1. The fans _ _ _ _ to be enjoying themselves!

2. Get the _ _ _ _ in the net.

5. The _ _ _ line runs through the center circle.

6. "He shoots, he _ _ _ _ _ _ !"

7. It's _ _ to kick the puck to a teammate.

8. Player's aim: _ _ _ _ _.

11. The Legion _ _ Doom.

13. Number of players on a team: _ _ _.

15. An illegal pass from one zone to another: _ _ _ _ _ _ _.

17. Mighty Ducks of _ _ _ _ _ _ _.

19. Hockey is a game of _ _ _ _ _ _.

20. Each face-off circle has a center _ _ _.

22. Hockey _ _ fun!

24. A popular drink with thirsty fans: _ _ _.

26. It's time to suit _ _ for the game.

Game 6

Odd Things Out

In each of these groups, one word just doesn't belong.
Can you spot the misfit?

shin pads
shinny
skates
helmet

pass
check
shoot
penalty

Devils
Flyers
Expos
Panthers

tripping
stand-up
inverted-V
butterfly

crease
blue line
center circle
slapshot

Upper Deck
Pinnacle
Leaf
Canadiens

Geezer Glory

The Toronto Maple Leafs won the Stanley Cup in 1967 with the oldest champs ever. Their average age was 31, and three were over 40.

Still, It Must Have Hurt!

Legend has it that Bobby Baun scored the Stanley Cup-winning goal for the Leafs in 1964 playing with a broken leg. In truth, it was only a cracked ankle bone.

Wayne's World

Quick—who's the greatest hockey player ever? It's a good bet some of you said Wayne Gretzky, right? No question, the Great One has scored an amazing number of hockey feats. How much do you know about the wondrous Wayne?

1. **Which of these NHL records did Gretz set? (You can choose more than one.)**
    (a) Scored the most goals in hockey history.
    (b) Earned the most points in hockey history.
    (c) Won the Rookie of the Year award in his first year with the NHL.
    (d) Scored points in the greatest number of games in a row.
    (e) Was the youngest player to net 50 goals in one season.
    (f) Scored the most goals in one season.

2. **What's unusual about his sweater?**
(a) He wears it inside out.
(b) It doesn't have his name on it.
(c) He tucks the right side into his pants.
(d) It says "The Great One" on the back.

3. **Why did he choose 99 for his player number?**
(a) It was the highest two-digit number possible.
(b) His coach suggested it.
(c) His father suggested it.
(d) The number was in his favorite Led Zeppelin song.

4. **What connection does Gretz have to Lady Byng?**
(a) She was his grandmother.
(b) She organized a benefit game he played in.
(c) He was once engaged to her.
(d) Her name is on a trophy he won.

5. **How many NHL teams has Wayne played for? Extra points if you can name them.**
(a) Two
(b) Three
(c) Four
(d) Five

More Hockey Lingo

Here's another chance to win points for hockey talk. Match these words with their definitions.

1. Butterfly

(a) The goalie is on his or her knees with legs spread outward.

(b) In this shot the puck soars through the air.

(c) The goalie's arms are held up like wings.

(d) A brightly colored winged insect.

2. Shinny

(a) A simple hockey game played outdoors

(b) A free shot on goal

(c) A pad covering the shins

(d) Getting hit on the shins with the puck

3. Shutout

(a) Arriving late to a game and not being allowed to go in

(b) A penalty that puts a player out of the game

(c) A game in which a goaltender stops all attempts by the opposing team to score a goal

(d) When a team does not get to the playoffs

4. The crease

(a) Regulation crease in players' pants

(b) The goalie's protected area in front of the net

(c) What happens to a player's jersey during a game

(d) The center circle

Game 9

She Shoots,
She Wins Olympic Gold!

The 1998 Winter Olympics in Nagano, Japan, proved to the world that women can stickhandle their way to a goal. In fact, women have played hockey ever since the game was organized more than 100 years ago. Up to the 1940s, women's hockey teams flourished in North America, attracting big crowds to their games. Then for a long time girls and women were discouraged from playing much, and hockey became mostly a man's game.

Now the girls are back! How much do you know about the way they play the game?

1. **What is the difference between women's and men's hockey? Choose all the statements below that apply.**
(a) Intentional body checking is not allowed in the women's game.
(b) Male hockey players are, on average, bigger and stronger.
(c) The women's game depends more on strategy and skillful moves than on muscle power.
(d) Female players never get into fights.

2. **Who were the Rivulettes?**
(a) A famous pop music trio of the 1950s
(b) A group that used to entertain during hockey intermissions
(c) A 1930s women's hockey team that won nearly every game it played
(d) The only women's hockey team to win the Stanley Cup

3. **Which women's team won hockey gold at the 1998 Olympics?**
(a) Canada
(b) United States
(c) Japan
(d) China

4. **How many women's world hockey championships did Team Canada win before the 1998 Olympics?**
(a) None
(b) One
(c) Two
(d) Four

5. **What is Manon Rhéaume famous for?**

(a) She scored the winning goal at Nagano.

(b) She is the first and only woman to play in the NHL.

(c) She is the captain of Team USA.

(d) She pretended to be a boy to play on a boy's team.

6. **How many countries have national women's hockey teams?**

(a) Two: Canada and the United States

(c) Four

(d) Six

(e) More than a dozen

7. **How is a woman's hockey uniform different from a man's?**

(a) It has more padding.

(b) It has an ankle-length skirt rather than shorts.

(c) It's exactly the same.

(d) It's proportioned to fit a woman's smaller, lighter body.

Who Is That Masked Man?

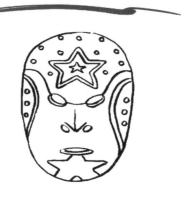

Back in 1959, Canadiens goalie Jacques Plante donned a mask and became the first NHL netminder to regularly wear one. No wonder—he had taken hits from flying pucks game after game. His nose had been broken four times; his cheekbones, jaw, and skull had been fractured; and he had received about 200 stitches to his face.

Some coaches thought that wearing a mask would interfere with a goalie's vision. They also thought that wearing a mask was not very macho. But the netminders had other ideas, and soon they were all wearing face protection. Today goalie masks are wild and wonderful works of art and are part of the spectacle of hockey.

No answers needed here, just your imagination. Color these masks any way you like and then design one of your own.

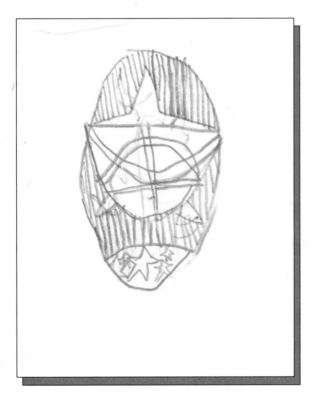

And the Winner Is...

In hockey, winning the game isn't everything—there's winning a trophy, too! Besides the grand prize for the NHL championship team, several other trophies are awarded each year for individual achievements.

How many of these trophies can you bag? Pick the right description for each one.

1. Hart Memorial Trophy
(a) Most valuable player to his team during the regular season
(b) Most points in international competition
(c) Flashiest skater

2. Lady Byng Memorial Trophy
(a) Most assists
(b) Sportsmanship and gentlemanly conduct
(c) Best haircut

3. Calder Trophy
(a) Rookie of the Year
(b) Best stickhandling
(c) Best attendance record

4. Art Ross Trophy

(a) Goalie with the most shutouts

(b) Most valuable player in the playoffs

(c) Highest scorer in one season

5. Vezina Trophy

(a) Best goaltender

(b) Best right winger

(c) Most original goalie mask

6. Stanley Cup

(a) Best player named Stanley

(b) Winners of most games that season

(c) NHL playoffs winners

Hats Off!

When Blackhawks captain Dirk Graham scored three goals—a hat trick—in the last game of the 1992 Stanley Cup finals, blissed-out Chicago fans tossed 311 hats onto the ice. Dirk got to keep all the hats.

Game 12
Reading the Signals

Who's the person on the ice everybody hates but can't do without? Right—the referee. He's the guy in the striped shirt making those funny moves with his arms. No, he's not scratching an itch or trying to keep warm—he's telling you something. Was it a goal or a miss? Was that player offside or on? What's happening in that pileup at the boards?

Match the signals shown on the next page with the meanings in the list below. Write the correct meaning on the line beneath each picture.

icing
disallowed goal
boarding
elbowing
cross-checking
hooking
high-sticking
charging
holding

(a) ___icing___   (b) ___disallow goal___   (c) ___hooking___

(d) ___holding___   (e) ___elbowing___   (f) ___cross checking___

(g) ___boarding___   (h) ___charging___   (i) ___high stiching___

Circle and Score!

This puzzle might look like a scramble, but hiding in it are 24 hockey terms and names of players. First figure out the words from the clues on the next page and then find and circle them in the puzzle. The words can run in any direction—horizontally, vertically, diagonally, backwards, or bottom to top—but always in a straight line. And sometimes they overlap—the same letter might be part of two or more words.

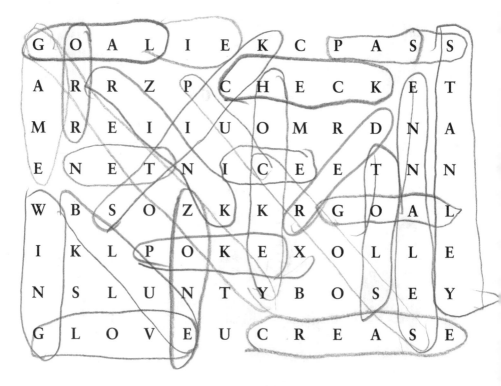

```
G  O  A  L  I  E  K  C  P  A  S  S
A  R  R  Z  P  C  H  E  C  K  E  T
M  R  E  I  I  U  O  M  R  D  N  A
E  N  E  T  N  I  C  E  E  T  N  N
W  B  S  O  Z  K  K  R  G  O  A  L
I  K  L  P  O  K  E  X  O  L  L  E
N  S  L  U  N  T  Y  B  O  S  E  Y
G  L  O  V  E  U  C  R  E  A  S  E
```

Clues

1. ~~Goal~~ *blue* line.
2. In men's and boys' hockey, it's OK to body-_check_
3. The area just in front of the net: _Crease._
4. It's against the rules to _Cross_-check an opponent.
5. Combining this word with the word for No. 21 gives you the major NHL trophy: _Cup_.
6. Hockey is a super-fast _Game_
7. Hand protection: _Glove._
8. It makes the fans cheer: _Goal_.
9. The _Goalie_ carries an extra-wide stick.
10. The Great One: _Gretzky_.
11. _Hockey_ began in Canada more than 100 years ago.
12. Hockey's playing surface: _Ice_.
13. Aim for the _Net_
14. Former star defenseman Bobby _Orr_
15. If you _pass_ to a teammate who scores, you get an assist.
16. Type of stick check: _poke_
17. The _red_ line runs through the center circle.
18. Hockey is played on a _rink_.
19. "The Finnish Flash": _Selanne_.
20. Area between the defensive zone face-off circles: _Slot_.
21. Goes with No. 5: _Stanley_.
22. It's against the rules to carry your _stick_ above your shoulders.
23. Each team has a left and a right _wing_
24. Your team's goal is in your defending _zone_.

Still More Hockey Lingo

Suit up for another hockey-talk game. Match these terms with their definitions.

1. **Breakaway**
   (a) Breaking out of a scramble
   (b) A fight
   (c) When a puck carrier breaks in alone on the goalie
   (d) A helmet with a visor attachment

2. **Neutral zone**
   (a) The center area between the blue lines
   (b) The area behind the nets
   (c) A face-off circle
   (d) A 0.6-meter (2-foot) area around the perimeter of the rink

3. **Power play**
   (a) Brilliant stickhandling by the team's star forward
   (b) A strong defensive play
   (c) When a team has a really good night
   (d) When one team has an extra player on the ice because a player on the other team is in the penalty box

visor?

4. Sudden death

(a) Overtime play in which the first team to score wins the game

(b) Missing a penalty shot

(c) A huge fight that ends the game

(d) When the netminder stops a goal that would have won the game

5. Penalty killing

(a) When a player gets so many penalties that he or she feels "killed"

(b) Special plays to cope with being one player short because of a penalty

(c) Trying to "kill" the opposing team by hitting, slashing, and other illegal moves

(d) Trying to get the other team to rack up penalties

The Name of the Game

There's power in a name. Imagine if your team were called the Wet Noodles—how many goals do you think you could slam into the net? But if your name were the Horrible Ghastly Alien Killer Monsters, you'd probably score big time.

Well, maybe it's not quite that simple. But here's a name game that'll let you rack up serious points.

1. List at least two NHL teams whose names fit into each of these groups:

(a) Four-footed animals

(b) Birds (flying or nonflying)

(c) Natural disasters

(d) Job descriptions or titles

(e) Names that mean "Canadians"

2. Which team is named after a prehistoric animal?

3. Which team is named after a sea creature?

4. Which team's name means a type of music?

5. Which team's name came from a movie?

The Disappearing Rover

The first hockey teams had seven players on a side. The seventh man was called a rover.

Not a Shy Guy

As a publicity stunt, Eddie Shore, a Bruins star defenseman of the 1920s and '30s, once skated out onto the ice wearing a cape and blowing kisses to the crowd as the band played "Hail to the Chief," a piece normally played to honor U.S. presidents.

Scramble!

To win this game, you've got to get into some scrambles. First, find the right words to complete each of the statements below. The answers are right there in brackets at the end of each statement—except that they're all in a jumble. Unscramble the letters and write the correct words on the lines.

Hint: Can you spot a hidden clue to one of the answers?

1. The _____ in Toronto is an entertainment center that celebrates hockey's history and heroes. (**cHeyko lalH of meaF**)

2. The C on the front of some players' jerseys stands for _____. (**anticpa**)

3. A _____ pass is a good way to get the puck to a teammate behind you. (**chaadnkb**)

4. The only Russian-trained player to be elected to the Hockey Hall of Fame is Vladislav _____. (kitTera)

5. The linesmen are easy to spot in their _____ jerseys. (dristep)

6. The Sabres' Dominik Hasek is the superstar _____ who helped his native Czech Republic win hockey gold at the 1998 Winter Olympics. (otdrgaeeln)

7. For scoring goals, _____ is more important than power. (pedse)

8. In junior hockey, all players must wear _____. (amssk)

9. The first team in the 1990's to win two Stanely Cups was the _____. (brigthusPt nePusing)

10. If a player falls over your stick, you could get a penalty for _____. (grinpipt)

But the Leafs Don't Wear Kilts

Bagpipes are played to open each NHL season at Toronto's Maple Leaf Gardens.

Game 17

Minor League Tryout

No big stars, plays, or rules in this quiz—it's just a collection of fun facts. Pick the right answer for each.

1. **How many sticks does each NHL player go through, on average, per season?**
   (a) 5 to 10
   (b) 20 to 50
   (c) 100 to 200
   (d) More than 300

2. **What's the average height and weight of an NHL player?**
   (a) 175 cm (5 ft. 9 in.) and 77 kg (170 lbs.)
   (b) 180 cm (5 ft. 11 in.) and 83 kg (184 lbs.)
   (c) 185 cm (6 ft. 1 in.) and 89 kg (196 lbs.)
   (d) 190 cm (6 ft. 3 in.) and 100 kg (220 lbs.)

3. **What is inscribed on the inside of the Stanley Cup?**
   (a) The names of the Cup champions of 1907 and 1915
   (b) The names of all the winning teams in cup history
   (c) "Congratulations, chaps!"
   (d) "This cup was donated by Lord Stanley of Preston."

4. **What was shown on the POGs issued by the NHL in 1995?**
(a) Crests of all the teams in the league that year
(b) Player pictures and statistics
(c) Coaches, referees, and linesmen
(d) Scenes from famous games

5. **What do hockey cards show?**
(a) Player pictures, biographies, and stats
(b) Regular playing cards with hockey stars on the backs
(c) Scenes from famous games
(d) Stars of the past on one side, today's stars on the other

Star Challenge

This time, search for the stars. The names of 14 NHL players and teams are included in this crossword. Figure out the clues first and then write the words in the puzzle. This one's tricky, so the words are listed at the top of the next page in alphabetical order.

all	Coyotes	gear	L.A.	OK
at	Cup	get	Leafs	Roy
bid	Devils	Jagr	Mats	San
Blues	film	John	Miller	Teemu
Bure	Flyers	Kariya	net	tip

Across

2. *The Mighty Ducks* is a Disney _ _ _ _.
4. _._. Kings.
8. _ _ _ _ _ Selanne.
10. Toronto Maple _ _ _ _ _.
12. A hot _ _ _ for rookies: practice your skating.
14. The Mighty Ducks' Paul _ _ _ _ _ _.
15. The St. Louis _ _ _ _ _.
18. Czech-born star Jaromir _ _ _ _.
21. Pavel _ _ _ _.
22. The Phoenix _ _ _ _ _ _ _.
23. The New Jersey _ _ _ _ _ _.

Down

1. _ _ _ -star team.
3. Leafs captain, _ _ _ _ Sundin.
5. Shoot the puck into the _ _ _.
6. The Stanley _ _ _.
7. Pads and skates are hockey _ _ _ _.
9. Coach of Canada's 1998 Olympics women's hockey team, Shannon _ _ _ _ _ _.
11. The Philadelphia _ _ _ _ _ _.
13. It's _ _ to pass the puck.
16. _ _ _ Jose Sharks.
17. Superstar goaltender Patrick _ _ _.
18. Philadelphia Flyers' _ _ _ _ LeClair.
19. _ _-home game.
20. Hope you _ _ _ a goal!
21. Make a _ _ _ to trade a player.

Stars of Ice and Screen

Two NHL players, Basil McRae and Mike Modano, appeared briefly (as themselves) in the 1992 movie The Mighty Ducks.

History Lesson

The Montreal Canadiens are the No. 1 NHL champs, winning the Stanley Cup 24 times. The Toronto Maple Leafs are runners-up with 11 wins.

Hockey's Best LIne?

"I went to a fight and a hockey game broke out." Comic Rodney Dangerfield said it on *The Tonight Show* starring Johnny Carson in 1983.

Game 19

Jazzy Jerseys

One of the great things about playing hockey is the gear you get to wear. Slip the team jersey over your pads and you look not only amazing but really HUGE!

Here are some famous jerseys from the present and past. Write the name of the team on the line beside the picture of each jersey. You could try adding the teams' colors, too.

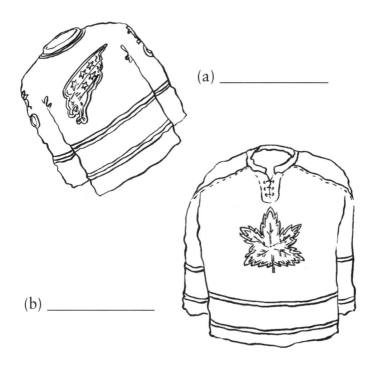

(a) _____

(b) _____

(c) _____

(d) _____

(e) _____

(f) _____

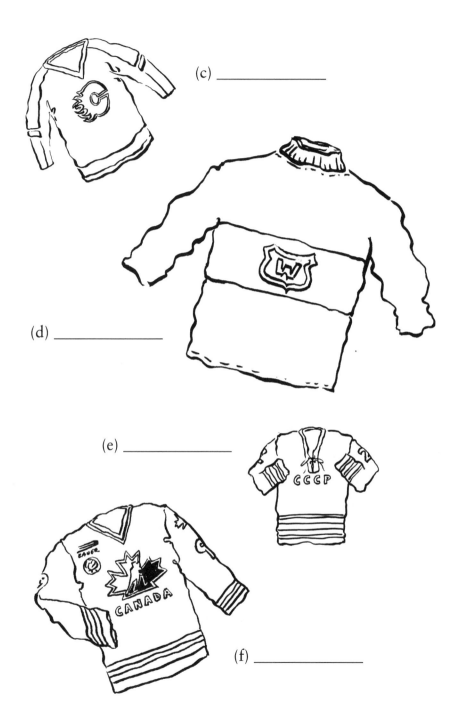

Making the Moves

When it comes down to it, hockey consists of four basic skills—skating, stickhandling, passing, and shooting. (Hammering your opponent into the boards is an extra.) So skate right up to center ice and test your knowledge of hockey moves and plays. Answer true or false by writing T or F on the line after each statement.

1. Shooting is the most important skill in hockey. ____
2. The best way to stop is to glide into the boards. ____
3. You skate backwards using C-shaped strides. ____
4. The crossover is a good way to skate forward quickly.___
5. Stickhandling means the way you hold your stick. ____
6. You should keep your eyes on the puck when you're carrying it. ____
7. If you pass to a teammate who scores, both of you get a point. ____
8. If your pass hits the boards, you get a penalty. ____
9. When receiving a pass, you should hold your stick very firmly. ____
10. The first shot to master is the slapshot. ____
11. Players who shoot the puck hardest score the most goals. ____
12. The slapshot backswing is like a golf swing. ____

Hockey Lingo Playoffs

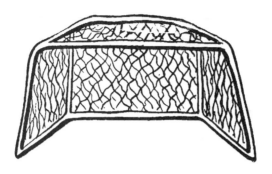

Here's your chance to smash in a winning goal with this last group of hockey terms and nicknames. Pick the correct definitions.

1. Series of the Century

(a) Stanley Cup playoffs of 1995

(b) 1972 Summit Series between the Soviet National Team and Team Canada

(c) Canada Cup series of 1991

(d) Men's hockey competition at the 1998 Winter Olympics

2. Legion of Doom

(a) Canadiens stars of the 1950s Maurice (Rocket) Richard and his brother Henri (Pocket Rocket)

(b) Eric Lindros, Mikael Renberg, and John LeClair

(c) The Colorado Avalanche

(d) Joe Sakic, Doug Gilmour, and Scott Stevens

3. Power forward

(a) Putting the most powerful player up front

(b) A big, rugged scorer

(c) A power play in which all players skate forward in a rush

(d) Stickhandling the puck toward the net very powerfully

4. Original Six

(a) The first six teams to win the Stanley Cup

(b) The first six teams in the NHL

(c) Montreal Canadiens, Toronto Maple Leafs, Detroit Red Wings, Chicago Blackhawks, Boston Bruins, and New York Rangers

(d) The first six European countries to have national hockey teams

5. MVP

(a) Most valuable player

(b) Most vicious player

(c) A "moving-V" play

(d) Maurice Vladimir Poirot, Canadiens star forward of the 1950s

6. D-man

a) New Jersey Devils player

b) Worst player on a team

c) A goalie who likes to dive onto the puck

d) Defenseman

Masks Are a Lot Better Now

Jacques Plante was the first goalie to wear a mask regularly, but he wasn't the first to put one on in a game.

Clint Benedict of the Montreal Maroons wore a crude leather mask for a few games in 1930 after suffering a broken nose from a flying puck. But when the mask was jammed into his face in a scramble, causing another injury, he tossed the thing aside and decided to retire from hockey.

Maybe Mars Has a Team

"We're losing at home; we can't win on the road. My failure as a coach is that I can't figure out anyplace else to play." Former coach Harry Neale once said this, proving that hockey coaches have a sense of humor.

Answers

Game 1
Rink-O-Rama

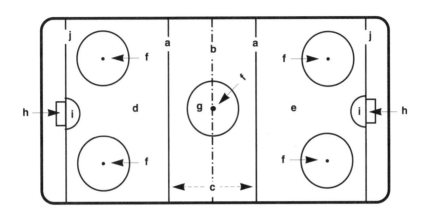

(a) blue line   (e) attacking zone   (i) goal crease
(b) centerline   (f) face-off spot   (j) goal line
(c) neutral zone   (g) center-ice circle
(d) defending zone   (h) goal

Game 2
Team Plays

1. Calgary Flames, Montreal Canadiens, Toronto Maple
   Leafs, Vancouver Canucks, Edmonton Oilers, Ottawa Senators

2. (a) Buffalo Sabres, (b) New Jersey Devils, (c) Detroit Red
   Wings, (d) Boston Bruins, (e) Pittsburgh Penguins,
   (f) Chicago Blackhawks

Game 3
Playing by the Rules

1. (a) No. A red light signals a goal. A green light signals the end of a period or game. These lights are set up behind each net.

   (b) Yes. Frozen pucks bounce less and fly along the ice faster than thawed ones. For this reason, the linesmen place the puck on the ice during time-outs rather than holding or pocketing it.

   (c) Yes—except in Europe, where ice rinks are wider, measuring about 61 meters by 30.5 meters (200 feet by 100 feet).

   (d) No. Hockey has three periods of 20 minutes each. (But before 1910, two 30-minute periods was, in fact, the rule.)

   (e) No. The boards should be no higher than 1.2 meters (4 feet).

   (f) Yes, and a good thing too. Before this rule was passed in1965–66, penalty servers of both teams sat together, making it easy for them to continue the fight that put them there in the first place.

2. (a) No. It's OK as long as you drop the puck right away.

   (b) Yes. The other team gets a penalty shot (free shot).

   (c) Yes. It's called holding.

   (d) Yes. This rule has gone back and forth in pro hockey. In 1979 a rule was made that NHL players had to wear helmets, but in 1992 protective headgear became optional. Now it's the rule again.

46

(e) Yes. It's called high-sticking.

(f) Yes. Netminders used to be allowed to stop pucks by diving onto them out of the goal area, but the rule was changed in 1959–60 when Canadiens goalie Jacques Plante got very good at this and would freeze the puck long enough to stop play.

(g) Yes. Back in the 1960s, some sneaky players would cut holes in their gloves big enough to get their fingers or even their fists through. They could then grab onto opponents' jerseys to stop them, or even throw an illegal punch the referees couldn't see.

(h) Yes, it's called icing. This rule has several exceptions, though. For example, if you score a goal doing this, it's not icing—it's a great shot!

(i) Yes. This one is called offside.

(j) You bet. According to the *National Hockey League Official Rules*, starting a fight earns a game misconduct, and wearing face protection while doing so rates an extra two-minute penalty. Face shields can be dangerous weapons in a fight.

Game 4
Hockey Lingo

1. (c) A fast, powerful shot made with a swinging stroke. This shot's got flash.

2. (d) An ice-cleaning machine. A Zamboni first cleaned the ice in a game at the Montreal Forum on March 10, 1955.

3. (b) A player scores three times in a game. Wayne Gretzky has made the most hat tricks so far. He's scored at least three goals in 35 games.

4. (c) The glove a goalie wears on his or her stick hand.

5. (c) To maneuver the puck with your stick. Good stickhandling is a basic hockey skill.

Game 5
Cross-Check

Game 6
Odd Things Out

1. Shinny is an informal hockey game played outdoors on ice or pavement. The other words refer to hockey players' equipment.

2. A penalty is what you get if you break a hockey rule. The other words refer to hockey moves.

3. The Expos are a baseball team. The other words are names of hockey teams.

4. Tripping is an illegal action in hockey. The other words describe goalie positions.

5. A slapshot is a hockey play. The other words refer to parts of a hockey rink.

6. The Canadiens are the Montreal hockey team. The rest refer to hockey card companies.

Game 7
Wayne's World

1. Gretzky set all these records except (c). Here are the stories:

(a) In 1994 Gretz scored his 802nd goal, beating the former career record set by his idol, Gordie Howe.

(b) He set a 1,851-point record in 1989. In 1995, he reached 2,500 points.

(c) Nope. Although Gretz racked up 137 points in his first year with the NHL (1979–80) and won the most valuable player award (Hart Memorial Trophy), he was declared not eligible for the rookie award (Calder Trophy) because he'd already played one season as a professional in a different league, the WHA (World Hockey Association).

(d) He scored in 51 straight NHL games in 1983–84, totalling 61 goals and 92 assists.

(e) He was 19 years and 2 months when he scored 50 goals in his first NHL season.

(f) Wayne netted 92 goals in the 1981–82 season.

2. (c) He tucks the right side into his pants. Wayne was only 6 when he started playing with 10-year-olds in a Brantford, Ontario, atom league. His oversize sweater kept getting caught on his stick handle, so he did the smart thing. Now he uses Velcro to make sure his sweater stays tucked.

3. (b) His coach suggested it. Wayne was 16 when he began playing junior hockey for the Soo Greyhounds in Sault Ste. Marie, Ontario. He wanted No. 9, his hero Gordie Howe's number, but another player was already wearing it. When his coach suggested 99, Gretz agreed, and he went on to make the number famous.

4. (d) Her name is on a trophy he won. Wayne won his first Lady Byng Memorial Trophy for sportsmanship in 1980. Since then, he's netted three more.

5. (c) Four. Edmonton Oilers, Los Angeles Kings, St. Louis Blues, New York Rangers.

Game 8
More Hockey Lingo

1. (a) The goalie is on his or her knees with legs spread outward. In this position, the goalie covers the greatest amount of ice surface.
2. (a) A simple hockey game played outdoors. Lots of kids practice their hockey skills in shinny games, on ice, or with a ball on pavement.

3. (c) A game in which a goaltender stops all attempts by the opposing team to score a goal.

4. (b) The goalie's protected area in front of the net. This is a marked-off, semicircular area painted light blue.

Game 9
She Shoots, She Wins Olympic Gold!

1. (a), (b), and (c). Body checking was banned in women's hockey in 1990. As a result, women count on speed and skillful moves to score. Men are generally bigger and stronger than women, and their game emphasizes power. As for fighting, some women players enjoy body checking, so who knows how their game may change in the future?

2. (c) A 1930s women's hockey team that won nearly every game it played. This remarkable team from Preston, Ontario, lost only 2 of the 350 games it played.

3. (b) United States.

4. (d) Four. Canada has won every women's world championship, in 1990, 1992, 1994, and 1997.

5. (b) She is the first and only woman to have played in the NHL. In 1992, Canadian Manon Rhéaume played in an exhibition game for the Tampa Bay Lightning.

6. (e) More than a dozen. So far, the most advanced teams are from Canada, the United States, Japan, Finland, Russia, Germany, China, Sweden, and Switzerland.

7. (d) It's proportioned to fit a woman's smaller, lighter body. Women's outerwear is much the same as men's but is shaped to fit. When proper gear is not available, however, lots of

girls and women borrow from the guys. And, amazingly, women hockey players at the turn of the century did indeed wear ankle-length skirts.

Game 11
And the Winner Is . . .

1. (a) Most valuable player to his team during the regular season
2. (b) Sportsmanship and gentlemanly conduct
3. (a) Rookie of the Year
4. (c) Highest scorer in one season
5. (a) Best goaltender
6. (c) NHL playoffs winner

Game 12
Reading the Signals

(a) icing, (b) disallowed goal, (c) hooking, (d) holding, (e) elbowing, (f) cross-checking, (g) boarding, (h) charging, (i) high-sticking

Game 13
Circle and Score!

1. blue, 2. check, 3. crease, 4. cross, 5. Cup, 6. game, 7. glove, 8. goal, 9. goalie 10. Gretzky, 11. hockey, 12 ice, 13. net, 14. Orr, 15. pass, 16. poke, 17. red, 18. rink, 19. Selanne, 20. slot, 21. Stanley, 22. stick, 23. wing, 24. zone

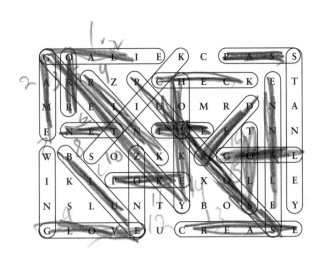

Game 14
Still More Hockey Lingo

1. (c) When a puck carrier breaks in alone on the goalie.
2. (a) The center area between the blue lines.
3. (d) When one team has an extra player on the ice because a player on the other team is in the penalty box. Teams try to take advantage of having this extra strength.
4. (a) Overtime play in which the first team to score wins the game.
5. (b) Special plays to cope with being one player short because of a penalty. A team brings out its best players to thwart the other team's power-play situation.

Game 15
The Name of the Game

1. (a) Boston Bruins, Florida Panthers, Phoenix Coyotes
   (b) Mighty Ducks of Anaheim, Pittsburgh Penguins. Half points for Detroit Red Wings or Chicago Blackhawks.

(c)   Colorado Avalanche, Carolina Hurricane

(d)   Ottawa Senators, New York Rangers,
        Los Angeles Kings, Edmonton Oilers

(e)   Montreal Canadiens and Vancouver Canucks

2. Nashville Predators. Their crests show the saber-toothed tiger.

3. San Jose Sharks

4. St. Louis Blues

5. Mighty Ducks of Anaheim. The movie, of course, was
   Disney's *The Mighty Ducks*.

Game 16
Scramble!

1.   Hockey Hall of Fame

2.   captain

3.   backhand

4.   Tretiak

5.   striped

6.   goaltender

7.   speed

8.   masks

9.   Pittsburgh Penguins

10. tripping

As for the hidden clue, it's actually right out in the open.
The answer to the first statement appears in No. 4.